The 10 Commandments Explained

By Silvia Vecchini
Illustrated by Antonio Vincenti

Pauline
BOOKS & MEDIA
Boston

Contents

1st Commandment
I am the Lord your God; you shall not have other gods besides me.

Who is God?
God is the one who makes himself found when I search for him. When I call him, God answers. He remains near to me at all times. My steps are directed toward you, O Lord. Teach me how to be truly free. Take your rightful place, God, at the center of my life.

The first place

God knows that we can be happy only if we are free. That is why he chose to create us as free persons with the ability to make our own choices. Unfortunately, we often forget that **freedom is God's precious gift** to us, one that we must guard and protect. Our freedom is fragile, just as we are fragile. At times, we put our liberty in danger by looking for happiness in things that don't last.

The Bible describes God as a "jealous" and "passionate" God. That is, God's **"heart" beats** with love for us, and he wants our hearts to beat for him.

God gives us the first commandment because he loves us and wants us to be free. The first commandment reminds us that a heart that puts God in first place is a heart that is truly free. When we recognize the importance of something, we can give it the proper significance. Then we will know how to make wise choices.

Liberator

Before even giving Moses the Tablets of the Law, the Ten Commandments, God presents himself to the Hebrew people and says, "I am the Lord, your God, who has brought you out of the land of Egypt, out of the house of slavery" (Ex 20:2).

The God who speaks in the Ten Commandments has listened to the cries of his people enslaved in Egypt. He has seen their suffering and has sent Moses in order to set them free.

God does not give us a law we cannot understand, nor does he demand what is unfair. God wants us to live **freely**. He says to us, "Listen! I have come to liberate you; I will show you how to no longer be slaves!" Before pronouncing the Ten Commandments, God wants us to remember that he is **a God who frees us to do what is good, saves us from sin and death, and loves us.** Those who have confidence in this truth can begin to walk the way of the Commandments.

You will NOT have other gods. . . . What does that mean?

The first commandment forbids superstition, magic, witchcraft, Satanism, and other things that could take the place of God in our hearts.

But what are idols? The word "idol" comes from the Greek language and means "image," "figure," or "representation." An idol is not what it appears to be; it is a deception!

It is important for each one of us to reflect on any "idols" in our lives and on their **influence** over us. Money, power, our appearance, having certain kinds of clothes or material goods, winning at all costs in sports, not missing a single episode of a certain TV program, playing video games every day—so many things can take God's place in our heart. Sometimes we even start to believe that it would be impossible to live without theses things.

Jesus and the 1ˢᵗ Commandment

One day a scribe questioned Jesus about this commandment. He asked, "What is **the first of all the commandments?**" Jesus responded, "The first is: Hear, O Israel! The Lord our God is the one Lord; you will love the Lord your God with all your heart and with all your soul, with all your mind and with all your strength" (Mk 12:28–30).

Another time, Jesus wanted to help us understand how important it is to reserve the first place in our lives for

If we entrust our happiness to any idol, we become "slaves" without even realizing it. God teaches us to open our eyes and distance ourselves from idols so that we can be free! Recognizing that God is our only Lord places us on the right path.

The Old Testament words help us understand the first commandment even more deeply. In fact, we can also translate the commandment this way: "You will not have other gods near me." We do not usually replace God with an idol, such as saying, "I don't have room for God, only for sports!" But we often do put something else "next to" God, almost as if it were his equal! God asks us to remember that the first place in our hearts **is reserved only for him**. All the rest comes after him. Put in their proper place of importance, other things can be part of our lives in a way that is good for us.

God, especially when it comes to money. Jesus first told a story as an example and then said, "No one can serve two masters, because he will hate the one and love the other, or love the one and hate the other. You cannot serve God and riches" (Lk 16:13).

The prophets taught the Israelites to be careful not to have **"divided" hearts**. At times, we too divide our hearts between God and something else. We may pretend that we have given our whole hearts to God, when we really have only given him part!

When we place God at the center of our whole heart, we give our lives deep roots. In that way, we are able to **grow like strong trees** do, and resist the storms that come our way.

Notebook

✓ What do you consider an idol that should be avoided, or something you've allowed to influence your choices too much? Write them down here.

✓ Have you ever experienced the freedom that comes from turning away from "idols"? If so, when?

✓ Ask God for the grace to remember Jesus's words and turn your life toward God, putting him in first place!

The Lord our God is the only Lord; you will love the Lord your God with all your heart and all your soul, with all your mind and all your strength.

My heart is the deepest part of who I am and where my ability to make choices is found.

My soul is my very life. It includes all my feelings.

My mind is home to my thoughts and intelligence.

My strength includes my body and my health.

2nd Commandment
You shall not take the name of the Lord your God in vain.

Let me know your name, Lord, and help me to understand who you are and who I truly am. Show me how to treat your name with reverence. Help me to understand that I am like a letter you have written and signed: whenever I keep your commandments, I bring your name to others.

The importance of a name

Each person's name has special importance. Our names identify who we are. From the perspective of the Bible, however, a name is something even more: it reveals the person who carries it, and announces his or her **role** or mission.

In a way, a person's name "is" the person. It reveals to others the deepest "self" of the one who bears it. Because of this, certain people we read about in the Bible received a **new** name at the moment in which their life changed.

When Jesus called Simon to discipleship, he gave Simon the new name "Peter," which means "rock." As the first "rock" of the Church, Peter was given the mission to provide a foundation for believers in Christ and guidance in living the faith.

The name of God is . . .

What is God's name? Before the time of Moses, the Hebrews did not have a name for God. Instead, they referred to him as the God of Abraham, Isaac, and Jacob. When Moses came, God revealed his name out of the burning bush as "**YHWH**." This name is not pronounced by the Jewish people out of reverence. The words "Lord," "Almighty," "Holy One," and other expressions are substituted for the sacred name of God. The name that God revealed to Moses means **"I am who I am"** (Ex 3:14). What does this name tell us? That God is present in our lives, attentive to our prayer, and ready to save us.

In his preaching, Jesus revealed something new to his disciples, telling them, "When you pray say, 'Our Father. . . .'" If you stop to think about it, it is amazing that we call God "**Father**"! This relationship expresses who God is, his nature. As Father, God has given us life; he provides for us, **he knows us, and he loves and forgives us.** We are called to act as brothers and sisters, and to think of ourselves as being under the gaze of the same Father.

Also, we are baptized "in the **name** of the Father, and of the Son, and of the Holy Spirit." We recall this whenever we say the name of the **Trinity** and make the Sign of the Cross.

Do NOT take God's name in vain. . . . What does that mean?

The second commandment forbids saying God's name in vain. This includes cursing, using vulgar language associated with the name of God, speaking about God disrespectfully, or making a false oath or a false promise.

But the second commandment also teaches us to guard against using God's **name** in a thoughtless way or for no reason. And there is the possibility of using God's name to make people feel guilty and do something that **you**—not God—want them to do. Deceiving others in this way is using God's name for one's own selfish interest.

Sometimes we abuse God's name by treating it as if it were some kind of **good luck charm**. Maybe we remember God only when there is an important event, school assignment, game, or something we want to go well for us. When we call on God in order to escape our responsibility, we use God's name in vain.

Jesus and the 2nd Commandment

Jesus himself speaks about this commandment and warns, "You have heard that it was said to those of ancient times, 'You shall not swear falsely. . . . But I say to you, Do not swear at all. . . . Let your word be 'Yes, Yes' or 'No, No'" (Mt 5:33, 34, 37). We must not make use of God's name to make ourselves look important. We must only speak

Words to think about

And finally, there is a truly misguided way of using God's name in vain: that is, to justify war in the name of God. No act of aggression or violence can be made right by claiming that it is the will of God, though many nations throughout history have tried to do so.

"No more violence! No more war! No more terrorism! May every religion bring justice and peace, forgiveness and life upon the earth. Love."

Saint John Paul II in Assisi in 2002

honestly and tell what we know without using God to give our words greater importance. Besides, Jesus affirms that it is not enough to "talk" about God if our actions don't reflect our words: **"Not everyone who says to me 'Lord, Lord,'** will enter the kingdom of heaven, but only the one who does the will of my Father in heaven" (Mt 7:21).

The best way to "speak" the name of God is to **do his will**. Jesus reminds us of this in the prayer he taught us, "Our Father in heaven, **hallowed be your name**. Your kingdom come. **Your will be done**, on earth as it is in heaven." (Mt 6:9–10).

Notebook

✔ Do you remember God throughout the day?

✔ Have there been occasions in which you felt closer to God?

Do you know the Prayer of the **Name of Jesus**? It is a way of prayer that is dear to Christians who belong to the Eastern Churches. The prayer is very simple: Jesus Christ, Son of God, have mercy on me, a sinner.

Try the prayer yourself or turn to Jesus with a brief phrase (for example: "Jesus, stay with me," or even, "Jesus, I believe in you"). While reciting the prayer, remain seated, stay still, and close your eyes. Repeat the words several times, slowly and softly, allowing them to touch the depths of your heart. Jesus's name means "the one who saves"!

✔ Try turning to Jesus with the Prayer of the Name, and then write or share about your experience of this prayer.

3rd Commandment
Remember to keep holy the Lord's day.

What good comes from hurrying or running about with school work, chores, or activities if I forget the meaning of celebration?

I search for you, Lord; opening my eyes, I find others. Now I ask myself who are my neighbors? What do they need? This is a new day; this is your day. I will stop in order to find the path again, and have within me the certainty that you will be near.

Remember . . .

This is the first commandment we find expressed in a "positive" way. God asks us to "remember" the day of rest. The Hebrew word used for "remember" can also be translated as "**guard**." The Lord's day is something precious that we are to guard with care.

For the Israelites this special day was and is Saturday, the seventh day, and is called the Sabbath. This is the day that God, having completed the work of creation, blessed and set apart; the day on which God rested. For Christians **the Lord's day is Sunday**. We gather in church on Sundays to celebrate the resurrection of Jesus. For us, every Sunday is a little Easter!

As Saint Jerome wrote in the 4th Century, "Sunday is the day of the Resurrection, it is the day of Christians, it is our day" (*Die Dominica Paschae* II, 52: CCL 78, 50). God invites us to guard this time: a time to rest, to worship him together, to enjoy the wonders of creation, to be alone as well as with the people we love. Sunday is truly a time to be free!

Resting . . . to be "more"

In the first book of the Bible, we read that after creating **man and woman**, God ceases his work and rests. God sets the seventh day apart.

But did God really need to rest?

This biblical verse teaches us that there is more to God than his creative acts; God "is" even if he doesn't "do," even if he rests. This day of celebration and rest calls us to remember that we, too, are more than just doers. The Sabbath gives us the space to **stop "doing" and to begin "being"**!

Each one of us is greater than what we can do. While at times we describe who we are by our habits, roles, or the activities in which we are involved, we should not forget the life of the spirit inside us. By setting aside Sunday for celebration and rest, we can recover this truth. A beautiful Jewish expression says that on the Sabbath day of celebration, it is as if God gives us "an extra soul," **a deeper and more intense breath of spiritual life!**

Keep holy. . . . What does that mean?

The third commandment asks us to keep our Sunday celebrations holy. But exactly how do you do this? To keep a day holy means **to set it apart**, to treat it differently from other days. We are called to live Sunday in a special way, remembering what unites us to our God and opens us to expressing gratitude for his gifts. Because of this, Christians are invited to **"come away"** from **regular habits**—for example, from the time we spend at work, in school, shopping—and enter into a different kind of time. This time is marked by "going out" from one's self and going toward

Jesus and the 3rd Commandment

In the Gospels we read that Jesus shocked and offended some Pharisees by healing the sick on the Sabbath day. They **accused** Jesus of breaking this commandment because work was not permitted on a day of rest and celebration, even if it was healing the sick! Their hearts were so hardened and without love that they saw the Sabbath as a set of harsh rules, and forgot about those who were weak and suffering, those who were asking for help on that day!

Jesus remembered that the third commandment was not just a duty but a gift. He answered them by saying, **"The sabbath was made for humankind, and not humankind for the sabbath"** (Mk 2:27). Jesus didn't go against the Law of Moses, but he others: coming together in church as a family in God's presence, listening to his Word, celebrating the Eucharist, praying for the needs of the world, helping those in difficulty—all that places **us in relationship with God and with our neighbor**. As this commandment is expressed in the Bible, God even wants the animals to rest. All living things are meant for more than producing!

The earth itself ought to rest! The third commandment invites us to guard all of creation, to respect what is too often used thoughtlessly or selfishly, to "give rest" to nature as a sign of our gratitude to the Creator, and to give praise to God for the beauty of his works!

reminded the Pharisees that people are more important than keeping the law in a way that does not even allow doing good! By answering in this manner, Jesus confirmed the heart of the commandment: God wants our life to be full, happy, and free. His commandments are made *for* us, not *against* us.

Jesus celebrated the Sabbath by healing someone in need so that person too could experience the joy of that day. Christians are called to live Sunday as a day of both celebration and sharing; we are to live joy in a way that makes us "**bringers**" of joy.

Notebook

✓ Do you live in a different way on feast days?

✓ What or who helps you to respect this commandment?

✓ A distinctive sign of the Christian Sunday is joy.
   What is your Sunday like?

Our union with Jesus at Sunday Mass is like a wave of love washing over us. This love wants to unite us not only with the people who are close to us but also with new people we meet.

In one of the documents of the Church we read, "If Sunday is a day of joy, Christians should declare by their actual behavior that we cannot be happy 'on our own'" *(Dies Domini, no 72).*

✓ Think about an act of kindness that you could do next week!
   Write it below.
   (Perhaps a phone call or a visit? An invitation to someone who may be alone? An hour of volunteer work somewhere?)

4th Commandment
Honor your father and your mother.

As the days
and seasons pass, I grow.
Years go by for my parents, too.
Teach me the secret of our bond.
Give me, my God, a happy heart
that is attentive and full of love.
There is something good in this
continuing chain: our family's
daily life together.

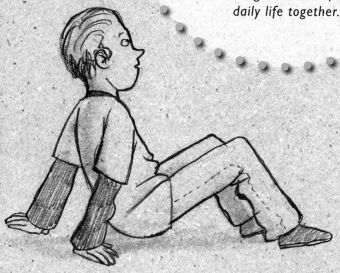

Father and Mother

This commandment, like the one before it, is expressed in a positive way. But the fourth commandment is different from all the rest, because it is followed by a promise. The book of Exodus says, "Honor your father and your mother, so that your days may be long in the land that the Lord your God is giving you" (Ex 20:12).

God **promises us goodness** and happiness. The honor we give to our parents will return to us in some way.

This commandment does not speak so much about the obedience we owe to our parents, but about something even more important.

God invites us to love our parents, to pay attention to them, and to show them respect through our words and actions.

But above all, he asks us **not to forget them** when they need us! When parents age, get sick, or experience particular need, their children must be there for them and not let their caring presence be absent.

There is no substitute for a child's affection and love.

The two tablets

Did you know there is a hidden key that can help us more fully understand this commandment? In the Bible, we read that God wrote his Ten Commandments on **two tablets of stone**. Saint Augustine grouped the Ten Commandments in this way: the first three (those which have to do with our relationship with God) he put on the first stone tablet. He grouped the other seven (which have to do with our relationships with others) on the second tablet.

The Jewish people, however, grouped the fourth commandment with those on the **first stone tablet.** They saw the honor we give to our parents as a duty done to the Lord. For them, honoring our parents meant honoring God as well!

Why? Because with God, our parents gave us life, something that we couldn't give to ourselves. This commandment helps us understand then that we are all creatures. It reminds us that God, our Creator, is a **Father and Mother** to each one of us.

To honor. . . .
What does that mean?

The fourth commandment speaks of helping our parents with the material things they need. It also encourages us to treat our parents and everyone who has rightful authority over us with a deep respect that comes from the heart. But what exactly does it mean to honor them?

To better understand, we can take a closer look at the verb "to honor." In Hebrew, this word is tied to the idea of giving weight to something, or treating it as something important.

Our parents—with their words, counsel, needs, and desires—ought to **"carry weight"** in our lives; they ought to count. We should not treat them lightly. The commandment teaches us to consider them with respect and "give proper weight" to them.

Jesus and the 4th Commandment

In one Gospel passage, Jesus strongly criticizes those who give excuses for not taking care of their parents in a dignified way. Jesus, however, also calls us to live freely in the community of those who believe in him. In this **"new" family** of God, we become related to each other and to Jesus through the Holy Spirit. In fact, Jesus once said, **"My mother and my brothers** are those who hear the word of God and do it" (Lk 8:21).

Still, there are no perfect parents. Some struggle with serious problems or sins. Others are—or choose to be—absent from their children's lives. Some parents cannot or do not adequately care for their children. And, sadly, there are parents who behave in ways that hurt the children God has entrusted to their care. What then?

Even if a mother or father acts in a dishonorable way, God asks us to honor them as much as we can from a safe place. We do that by trying to forgive them, by praying for them, and by becoming all that God created us to be.

Words to think about

A beautiful saying shows us the path to understanding our connection to our parents.

"Parents give two things to their children—roots and wings. The greatness and vigor of the wings depend on the depth and robustness of the roots."

Popular Proverb

This is not about loving one's own family less, but about opening our hearts to new ties and sharing with our neighbors. Jesus invites us not to close ourselves off from others, not to only consider our own family relationships, but to recognize that all the world's people are children of the same Father.

Notebook

✓ Do you express gratitude to your parents?
  Write down at least three ways you could do so from the heart.

✓ How is your relationship with your parents?

✓ What are some of the things you like most about your parents?

✓ When things in your family don't run smoothly what can you do
  to help the situation?

✓ Do you know how to forgive your parents?

Guarding the stories and traditions of your family is a way of honoring your parents. Ask them something about the past, talk together, and fill in the family tree below.

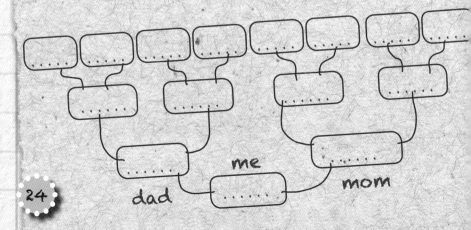

5th Commandment
You shall not kill.

Because each one of us is your image, God, no one is unimportant. No one can be done away with, removed, omitted, injured, put down, or eliminated. Help me to truly see you in my neighbor, and to recognize myself and you in every person.

Life is holy

For the Jewish people, this commandment addressed "getting even" or seeking revenge by taking someone's life. Taking the life of another person for any reason is always a very serious matter.

It might seem like this commandment is obvious, because it is already written in the **depths of our hearts**. But at the time in which the Ten Commandments were originally given, capital punishment and violent wars were common. And today? Unfortunately, we have not yet learned; we still kill one another!

We know this from what we read in newspapers and see on the television and internet news every day.

The fifth commandment reminds us clearly that life is sacred and that no one has the right to destroy it. In fact this commandment means that we have a responsibility to take care of our health by eating well, exercising, and not doing anything to harm or put ourselves in danger.

While breaking any of the other commandments leaves us with the possibility of reconciling or repairing a broken relationship, the act of killing does not. **Every person is unique and irreplaceable**. Even more, killing strikes at God because he created each individual person "in his image and likeness."

Enemy/brother

It is impressive to read the episode of the **killing of Abel** in the first few chapters of the Bible. It is as if we were warned against the tragic **consequences of hatred** from the very beginning of the human story. And the most impressive thing about this story is that the crime happens between two brothers!

Maybe the story about Cain and Abel teaches us that ending the life of another person always means ending the life of a **"brother."**

This reality of our being "brothers" and "sisters" ought to influence all our choices and considerations. Even in the midst of conflict and tension, we must stretch ourselves to use every way and resource to find a meeting point. Our creativity can help us discover how to dialogue and confront one another in a peaceful manner.

While taking a life is never a good thing, it sometimes happens during war, in an act of self-defense, or because of an accident. We can protect life by being peaceful, respectful, and careful regarding others.

5th Do NOT Kill. . . . What does that mean?

The fifth commandment is very direct and very brief! But this commandment asks that we open our eyes wide to reality and reflect on the fact that there are many ways to "take" someone's life.

Certainly, the most obvious way is by causing someone's death, and killing another person is the gravest wrong that anyone can do. But is refraining from killing anyone enough to keep this commandment? No. The fifth commandment invites us **to care for every human life**: that of a baby inside his or her mother's womb, waiting to be born; that of someone who is sick or of an elderly person nearing death; that of any brother or sister throughout the world who doesn't have necessities like food and water; even that of a criminal who has harmed others. The fifth commandment asks us to defend, protect, and promote life. Because all life comes from God, we should always choose life.

Jesus and the 5th Commandment

Jesus is very clear about this commandment. In the Sermon on the Mount he says, "You have heard that it was said to those of ancient times, **'You shall not murder'**; and 'whoever murders shall be liable to judgment.' But I say to you that if you are angry with a brother or sister, you will be liable to judgment" (Mt 5:21–22).

28

Words to think about

Not only should we not kill, Jesus tells us, but **we should not hate**. We should not call anyone "stupid" or any other insulting name, respond to another in anger or with indifference, or humiliate or mock anyone. All these things can deeply hurt and in some way "kill" or gravely harm another person.

When Jesus was arrested in the Garden of Gethsemane, Peter tried to defend him by pulling out his sword and striking the high priest's servant. Jesus disapproved of what Peter had done and healed the wounded man. Even in such a tragic moment, Jesus did not want his friends to respond to evil with violence. Jesus' words in the Gospel go even further, "**Love your enemies** and pray for those who persecute them, so that you may be children of your Father in heaven . . ." (Mt 5:44–45).

Notebook

V Jesus warns his disciples about violent words as well as actions.

Have you ever been wounded by a word, an insult, or a comment? When?

☐ yes   ☐ no

V Have you ever wounded someone by your words, actions, or by disregarding them?

☐ yes   ☐ no

Blessed Mother Teresa of Calcutta spent her whole life caring for and defending the lives of those who are the smallest and the neediest—the poorest of the poor. This poem is attributed to her.

> Life is an opportunity, seize it.
> Life is beauty, admire it.
> Life is a blessing, savor it.
> Life is a dream, make it a reality.
> Life is a challenge, face it.
> Life is a duty, accomplish it.
> Life is a game, play it.
> Life is precious, take care of it.
> Life is rich, conserve it.
> Life is love, enjoy it.
> Life is a mystery, discover it.
> Life is promise, fulfill it.
> Life is sadness, overcome it.
> Life is a hymn, sing it.
> Life is a struggle, accept it.
> Life is an adventure, risk it.
> Life is happiness, earn it.
> Life is life, defend it.

V What is life for you?

6th Commandment
You shall not commit adultery.

Love is your gift, Lord;
it fills the heart.
Love discovers new things and
reveals what has been hidden.
God, help me to be true,
loyal and faithful.
Help me to say with you:
I am for you.
You are for me.
Together we are one.

"One flesh"

The sixth commandment invites us to reflect on a reality that is important, wonderful, and mysterious: the bond existing between one man and one woman as husband and wife in married love.

In the Bible we read that husband and wife are called to be "one flesh": their union, which comes from God himself, is meant to be **deep, true, and between only the two of them.**

For this reason, anything that harms, endangers, or breaks this union is wrong. The relationship between husband and wife must be based on love, trust, and **faithfulness**.

The sixth commandment shows us that God is on the side of married couples, blessing them and guarding their loving union. So many things have changed since this commandment was given to us, that we might be tempted to think it is no longer in style!

And yet, our hearts do not change: men and women remain the same. Each one of us desires to be truly loved. Each one of us wants to be THE one—the only one—for the person we love.

Fake or honest?

The word "adultery" can be confusing. It has nothing to do with being an adult. Actually, "to adulterate" means **to falsify**, degrade, or weaken something. We say that contaminated food or medicine and weakened steel are "adulterated." But this word can be applied to relationships, too. We falsify a relationship, for example, if we act like we are someone's friend when we are not. We degrade and weaken a relationship when we do not fully respect ourselves or the other person. You may have noticed that sometimes people are considered valuable only when they are useful or have something someone else wants. This way of thinking treats people as if they were "things" or objects that can be taken at will and thrown away when they are no longer of use.

The sixth commandment motivates us to take another look at our friendships, to make sure that they are **respectful, authentic, and sincere**. The commandment invites us to look at our relationships and ask ourselves: are we faithful to others? Do we consider what is best for them? Do we respect their needs and feelings?

What do you want to be in your relationships with others: honest or a "fake"?

33

Do NOT commit adultery.... What does that mean?

The sixth commandment requires husbands and wives to keep the promise they made to each other and be faithful to their word. When a man and woman are married, they vow to be true to one another in good times and in bad, in sickness and in health. They promise to love and honor each other for the rest of their lives. Specifically, the sixth commandment forbids married people to cheat on each other by seeking romantic or sexual love outside their marriage.

This commandment, however, invites us to go beyond and recognize that sex is a **gift** that God intended *only* for marriage between one man and one woman. It is beautiful and authentic only when it expresses a love that is total, faithful, and for a lifetime. That is the kind of love marriage is. The sixth commandment warns us that those who separate sex from marriage lessen its meaning, wound themselves, and deeply hurt the other person. The sixth commandment teaches us to treat marriage with the dignity and respect it deserves and to avoid using our **bodies** and the bodies of others as objects.

Jesus and the 6th Commandment

In Matthew's Gospel we read that some Pharisees—who strictly followed the Law of Moses—questioned Jesus about divorce. Jesus answered by recalling the Genesis story, which describes God's creation of man and woman.

Jesus said, "Have you not read that the one who made them at the beginning 'made them male and female,' and said, 'For this reason a man shall leave his father and mother and be joined to his wife, and the two shall become one flesh'? So they are no longer two, but one flesh. **Therefore what God has joined together, let no one separate**" (Mt 19:4–6).

But the Pharisees argued back that in many cases, the Law of Moses allowed a man to divorce his wife.

Jesus then responded, "It was because you were so hard-hearted that Moses allowed you to divorce your wives, but **from the beginning it was not so**" (Mt 19:8).

Jesus knew how selfish we can be. He knew that our hearts can harden so much that we may deny love, break even our closest bonds, and close ourselves to the possibility of reconciliation.

But Jesus also knew that in God's heart, the marriage union has been **unbreakable** since the beginning. In God's eyes, a husband and wife have become "one."

Notebook

✓ People are not "objects": things to be used, taken when needed, forgotten when they are not convenient, and found again when you feel like it.

Have you ever displayed this kind of attitude toward another person?

Have you witnessed people being mistreated in these ways among your friends or at school?

☐ yes   ☐ no

✓ What do you think about this?

✓ In the Bible it is written that "the Lord does not see as mortals see, they look on the outward appearance, but the Lord looks on the heart" (1 Sam 16:7). What do you think about those who judge others based solely on appearance? Where does the value of a person truly lie?

In the creation story from Genesis we read that God created Eve from one of Adam's ribs. A Jewish commentary reveals the key to this story: "Woman came from the man's rib—not from his feet to be walked on, not from his head to be his superior, but from his side to be his equal . . . under his arm to be protected, and next to his heart to be loved."

from the *Talmud*

✓ Relationships between men and women ought to be based on respect, equality, and mutual enrichment. Reflect on some of the disrespectful or negative ways women and men are often presented in certain TV programs or advertisements.

7th Commandment
You shall not steal.

God, you have taught us that it is good to respect what belongs to others and to care for what belongs to all people. Honesty means not stealing or cheating. But you have shown us something even better and more beautiful than these things. Help me to give the way you do, to be generous, and to share unselfishly what belongs to us all.

A space of respect

The seventh commandment does not simply list specific things that should not be stolen. Like the fifth commandment, "you shall not kill," this commandment is brief, very clear, and absolute. We could perhaps reword it this way: "Do not take anything that belongs to your neighbor and not to you. Ever."

The seventh commandment forbids theft, which is taking for ourselves what **does not belong to us**.

Stealing something means breaking into someone else's personal space and committing an act of **injustice**. Even if the loss of property does not hurt someone physically, it leaves the person who was robbed with a lasting sense of humiliation and fear.

Anyone who breaks this commandment should not only ask for forgiveness, but should make **restitution**: that is, replace or pay for what was stolen.

The "theft" of freedom

Did you know that originally this commandment referred to stealing people's freedom and making them **slaves**? At the time in which the commandments were written, the slave trade was very profitable. It was necessary, therefore, to put a stop to the desire to get rich by selling people. Today, this meaning of the commandment may seem to be outdated. But is it really? In fact, there are over twenty-seven million slaves in our world today! If we just think of **children who are working** instead of going to school in so many countries; of those who are used by others unjustly and don't have the ability to change their situations; of young women who are forcibly kidnapped and "sold"—all these people are "slaves." Someone has "**robbed**" them of their liberty.

With this commandment, God once again takes the side of those who are weak and defends the rights belonging to every person.

Do NOT steal. . . . What does that mean?

Unfortunately, there are many ways to break this commandment. Here are only a few: people steal by not paying their taxes, by cheating on the prices they set, by not doing their own work, by spending money that was meant for someone else, by cheating, by getting rich in dishonest ways, by lending money but charging very high interest on it, and by paying less than what is owed to a worker.

If we reflect deeply, we understand that this commandment urges us to respect others by respecting what belongs to them and not to us. We should seriously consider how we treat all the "goods" that we share in common with others: public buildings, common spaces, means of transportation, etc. **Damaging** things that are for the use of people besides us breaks the seventh commandment. The **environment** we live in also falls into this category—nature, water, air. Every time these resources are plundered, stolen, or polluted, a serious theft is committed, because the earth's resources are intended for all of us.

Jesus and the 7th Commandment

At various moments in the Gospels, Jesus deals with the way in which we ought to consider the things we own. His words make us see this commandment from another perspective. They invite us to consider ourselves as "guardians" of the gifts we receive from the Lord and to become honest and generous "**stewards**" of them. In both little and great

Words to think about

The Earth is indeed a precious gift of the Creator who . . . has given us bearings that guide us as stewards of his creation.

Pope Benedict XVI General Audience Wednesday, August 26, 2009

Already today millions of people suffer and die in the world because they don't have fair access to resources like clean water. If the water is available, but people are not allowed to access it, this, too, is a very serious theft.

We are all called to be **stewards** of creation. That means we care for, protect, and develop the resources God has given us for the good of all people.

things, Jesus reminds us that we are called to **share what we possess** with our neighbor in need: "Whoever has two coats must share with anyone who has none; and whoever has food must do likewise" (Lk 3:11).

The seventh commandment involves much more than "not stealing." It means acting out of justice and taking responsibility for those who are near and also those who are far.

41

Notebook

✓ Have you ever taken something that wasn't yours? Have you been dishonest so that you could get something that didn't belong to you?

☐ yes   ☐ no

✓ Did you return what you took?

✓ Do you respect others' things? What about public goods or property?

Here are some things you can do to respect the seventh commandment when it comes to the environment and the resources that belong to everyone!

I turn off the light when I leave the room.
I do not leave machines on "stand-by."
I try not to waste water.
I throw garbage into a trash can.
I don't waste paper and I try to re-use paper by writing on both sides.
I respect plants and animals by taking care of them.
I choose to walk or bicycle instead of taking a vehicle when possible.
I recycle.
I learn more about the problem of clean water, and I do what I can so that it will someday become accessible to all people.

✓ Put a checkmark next to the things that you do regularly, and a dot near the things you want to try to do more often.

8th Commandment
You shall not bear false witness against your neighbor.

Lord, you give us the ability to speak. Our words can be warm and tender, full of sweetness and care; they can be playful and bring laughter; they can speak about friendship and make others feel how special they are. But words can also do harm. Guard me from using words that blaze and burn like dangerous fires. Keep me from using words that cut like knives. Help me, God, to remember how powerful words really are.

A climate of trust

The eighth commandment forbids lying or using words as weapons against others, and it invites us **to always tell the truth**. In our relationships with the people around us (family, friends, or at school), to speak falsely means breaking the trust we all depend on, the trust that makes it possible for us to live together.

The more honest and loyal we are with others, the stronger our confidence in each other will be. Trust helps our relationships to grow and allows us to live them peacefully. Even when situations are difficult and the problems we face are big, if there is trust, then everything becomes possible. We know that we **can count** on someone who will not betray us. This "climate of trust" will deepen and be safeguarded if we commit ourselves to being loyal to our neighbor and to "telling the truth" every day.

Sincere testimonies

When the eighth commandment was written, legal matters were decided in the open, often at the gates of the city before a judge and some witnesses. Originally the commandment was directed to these people because witness testimony often determined what would happen to someone who had been accused of a crime. Some cases carried very heavy penalties—including the death penalty. Not giving false testimony was extremely important then because **a person's life** hung in the balance.

Even in legal proceedings today, witnesses take an oath to tell the truth, because **truth and justice go together.** It is very important that those who are called to give testimony choose to tell the truth, even when doing so might make them "uncomfortable."

This commandment reminds us that words carry weight and have consequences. It warns us of the dangers of lying and reminds us that telling a "half-truth" is the same thing as telling a "**half-lie.**"

DO NOT give false testimony. . . .
What does that mean?

In the first place, the commandment calls us to never speak falsely "against" our neighbor, that is, not to damage, strike out at, or deliberately get someone in trouble. If we think about this commandment, it challenges us to reflect on how we use words. We should think carefully before engaging in **gossip**, the chitchat that goes from mouth to mouth spreading rumors and judgments about people, and **detraction**, which is exaggerating another's defects or limitations. Slander is another way to use words hurtfully. Slander is speaking in a way that damages someone's reputation. Using words in any of these harmful ways makes it more difficult for everyone to act freely. When we aren't free to be our true selves, we can wear "masks" that cover up or hide who we really are. It also goes against the eighth commandment to **flatter** others in order to take advantage of them or get something from them. Another kind of insincerity is encouraging someone in a wrong attitude or behavior, when it would be more honest and kind to help them change for the better.

Jesus and the 8th Commandment

Jesus invited his disciples to be truthful, sincere, and authentic when he said, "Be as innocent as **doves**" (see Mt 10:16).

Choosing truth is the first step to building **true and lasting relationships**. Truth gives others good reason to trust us.

Words to think about

A beautiful passage from Saint Augustine reminds us that God himself is Truth, and that Truth speaks to our hearts. We are all called to speak and act according to the truth.

"I understood that God is Truth. It is written, in fact, that God is light—not the light that our eyes see, but that which the heart sees, when it hears: God is the Truth."

Saint Augustine

Jesus asks those who follow him to use language simply, in a way that yes means yes and no means no. This honest way of speaking takes others into account and doesn't use words to wound. In an impressive passage of the Gospel, Jesus reminds us that our words come from whatever fills our hearts (see Mt 12:34).

If we tell lies, use words to make someone uncomfortable, or spread gossip, we cause all kinds of problems for ourselves and others. We not only wrong our neighbor, but we neglect our own "hearts" and remain unaware of what our hearts truly contain. Jesus encourages us to **choose** the good. He teaches us to guard our hearts as a treasure, since our words come from them. Jesus says, "The good person brings good things out of a good treasure, and the evil person brings evil things out of an evil treasure" (Mt 12:35).

Notebook

V It isn't always easy to tell the truth. Sometimes doing
so may mean going against the tide or risking yourself
in some way. Have you ever experienced this kind of
difficulty? Have you also known the beauty and sense of
freedom that come from telling the truth in a complicated
situation?

There is a well-known story, retold in different
ways that helps us to understand how serious gossip
is.

One day a woman who was a notorious gossip went to
an elderly priest for Confession. After he listened
to her attentively, the priest gave her a curious
penance: "Go home, take a pillow, climb to the roof,
and slash the pillow open with a knife. Then come
back to me." The woman, although surprised, did what
the confessor instructed her. When she returned
to him, he asked her: "What happened?" The woman
responded: "The pillow's feathers flew all over the
place!" Then the confessor said, "Now go and collect
all the feathers." "But that's impossible!" said the
upset woman. The priest looked at her knowingly and
said, "The same thing happens with the bad rumors
you spread. How can you ever take them back?"

V Have you ever spoken behind someone's back?

never   one time   many times   too often!

9th Commandment
You shall not covet your neighbor's wife.

Lord, you show us that true love is enough all by itself. When our love is real we don't look for other attention. God, give us real love that changes, grows, and renews itself. Teach us to know the difference between what looks or feels like love and what is genuine.

Do NOT covet. . . . What does that mean?

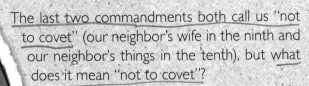

The last two commandments both call us "not to covet" (our neighbor's wife in the ninth and our neighbor's things in the tenth), but what does it mean "not to covet"?

Coveting is the uncontrolled **desire** that motivates people to become possessive of someone or something. This commandment warns us about what can happen inside our hearts, and invites us to focus our desires in good and healthy ways, and to respect people by **never treating them as objects** to use as we please.

Jesus and the 9th Commandment

As in other cases, here too the teachings of Jesus go "beyond" our initial understanding of this commandment.

Jesus, speaking to his disciples about the ninth commandment, says, "You have heard that it was said, 'You shall not commit adultery.' But I say to you that everyone who looks at a woman with lust has already committed adultery with her in his heart" (Mt 5:27–28).

When Jesus says, "You have heard that it was said . . . but I say to you," he does not mean, "I'm telling you something different." Rather, Jesus is saying, "I tell you the same thing but in a **deeper and more complete way.**"

It means respecting other friendships and relationships that already exist. This commandment can be applied to all people and every kind of relationship and friendship. It becomes even more important when we think about married people.

A married couple ought to be seen by others as a unique reality. **Husband and wife** share a bond all their own, a bond made of love, experiences, desires, needs, and tasks that no one ought to invade or threaten in any way.

Once again the center of everything seems to be the "heart." Jesus knows that our thoughts, desires, and feelings come from deep in our hearts. He invites us to be aware of what we find there.

Envy **begins** in the heart. It is almost as if we are counting what we don't have!

Jesus asks us instead to look within ourselves and the stories of our lives, to be thankful for what we do have and for the people close to us, and to focus our desire on **what has already been given to us**.

Notebook

✔ How do you act in friendships and in relationships? Are you a loyal person?

✔ What do you think of those who always seem to be searching for a new "love" or for more experiences or relationships?

✔ Can you explain how people cannot be "possessed," and at the same time should not be "stolen away"?

Look into your own heart, and think about the people you care about. Thank God for having given them to you.

Pledge to be loyal to the people in your life, never treating them as if they were objects to take away from someone else and always wanting what is truly best for them.

Write their names here:

Thank you, Jesus, for each one of these special people!

10th Commandment
You shall not covet your neighbor's goods.

Lord, what is
"enough"? Must I always
have more, buy more things,
and accumulate more possessions?
I know that I am more than what I have.
I know that my value is found in the
love that I can give. My God, help me
see clearly what has true value, what is
essential in life. Make me happy with
what you have given me and grateful for
all that I have. You know what I need.
Help me to trust in you.

Do NOT covet your neighbor's goods. . . . What does that mean?

Not to covet what belongs to your neighbor means not allowing yourself to be carried away by envy or greed. The tenth commandment warns against **the desire to have everything** immediately, to continuously have more, to gain at all costs, even when it means acting unjustly.

The tenth commandment is about material things, but it also has something to say about personal qualities, talents, positions or jobs, and awards.

Jesus and the 10th Commandment

Because he lived among us, Jesus has deeply personal knowledge of the human heart. He knows what it is to be anxious about **what we need** in order to live, and he understands our everyday concerns and fears.

This is what Jesus says to his disciples, "**Do not worry** about your life, what you will eat or what you will drink, or about your body, what you will wear. Is not life more than food, and the body more than clothing? Look at the birds of the air; they neither sow nor reap nor gather into barns, and yet your heavenly Father feeds them. Are you not of more value than they? Therefore do not worry, saying, 'What will we eat?' or 'What will

This commandment teaches that there is a "pure" way of thinking about things that belong to others: the first step in conquering the desire to have what belongs to others is learning to be grateful to God for our own lives and possessions.

Gratitude for what we have helps us to stop measuring ourselves against others, as if life were a kind of contest that is won by whoever has the latest style, the newest cell phone, or the "right" kind of house or car. Respecting this commandment means recognizing our own gifts and talents and making good use of them, while at the same time being happy when others make good and fruitful use of their gifts.

we drink?' or "What will we wear?' . . . and indeed your heavenly Father knows that you need all these things. But strive first for the kingdom of God and his righteousness, and all these things will be given to you as well" (Mt 6:25–26, 31–33).

Jesus wants us to be **free and confident**. He wants us to be free from worries about the future, which can seem to crush us at times. But Jesus also wants us to be free from "dependencies" on earthly goods. Jesus invites us to trust God and place the **richest treasure**—knowledge of God's love for us—at the center of our search.

"Make purses for yourselves that do not wear out, an unfailing treasure in heaven, where no thief comes near and no moth destroys. For where your treasure is, there your heart will be also" (Lk 12:33).

Notebook

✓ Are you envious of others because of what they possess?
Are you bitter about what you don't yet have?

never   sometimes   often

✓ Do you try to be grateful to God for all he has given you?
Write some of his gifts to you here:

✓ Are you able to be happy for the gifts God has given to others?

never   sometimes   often

Always wanting more can pit people against one another. Read how Jesus responds to two brothers who were fighting over an inheritance.

Someone in the crowd said to him, "Teacher, tell my brother to divide the family inheritance with me." But he said to him, "Friend, who set me to be a judge or arbitrator over you?" And he said to them, "Take care! Be on your guard against all kinds of greed; for one's life does not consist in the abundance of possessions" (Lk 12:13-15).

Jesus' words free us from the common way of thinking that we should always be ready to acquire or gain, even at the expense of others. Jesus' words help us understand the truth: our life and happiness do not depend on what we have, but on the love we share!

A New Commandment

We have read that Jesus did not come to do away with the Law but to fulfill the Ten Commandments in a deeper and more complete way.

In the Gospel of Mark Jesus says to his disciples, "The first [commandment] is, 'Hear, O Israel: the Lord our God, the Lord is one; you shall love the Lord your God with all your heart, and with all your soul, and with all your mind, and with all your strength.' The second is this, 'You shall love your neighbor as yourself.' There is no other commandment greater than these" (Mk 12:29–31).

Love of God and of neighbor is the center, the heart, of the Ten Commandments!

Saint Paul wrote, "Love is the fulfilling of the law" (Rom 13:10).

Jesus taught this in the words he preached; but even more, he showed us what this love looks like by how he lived on earth.

In the Gospel of John, we read what Jesus did at supper on the night he was arrested. With this gesture Jesus showed his disciples how to follow a **new commandment**.

"[Jesus] got up from the table, took off his outer robe, and tied a towel around himself. Then he poured water into a basin and began to wash the disciples' feet and to wipe them with the towel that was tied around him. After he had washed their feet, had put on his robe, and had returned to the table, he said to them, 'Do you know what I have done to you? You call me Teacher and Lord—and you are right for that is what I am. So if I, your Lord and Teacher, have washed your feet, you also ought to wash one another's feet. For I have set you an example, that you also should do as I have done to you. I give you a new commandment, that you love one another. Just **as I have loved you**, you also should love one another'" (Jn 13:4–5, 12–15, 34).

This is what is important and what Jesus asks of us: to love one another as brothers and sisters, to help and serve each other, to always choose humility and the strength that comes from what is truly good. . . .

The one **who loves like Jesus** keeps each of the Ten Commandments and makes them real in his or her life!

The Ten Commandments

1. I am the Lord your God; you shall not have strange gods before me.

2. You shall not take the name of the Lord your God in vain.

3. Remember to keep holy the Lord's day.

4. Honor your father and your mother.

5. You shall not kill.

6. You shall not commit adultery.

7. You shall not steal.

8. You shall not bear false witness against your neighbor.

9. You shall not covet your neighbor's wife.

10. You shall not covet your neighbor's goods.

The Ten Commandments . . . in positive terms!

After having learned the Ten Commandments in the traditional way, it is good to try to express them in "positive" language, too. This can help us better appreciate and understand the deeper messages that the commandments contain. Always remember that they are meant to point us toward goodness and happiness!

1. I will remember that you are my God, and I will put you in the first place in my heart.

2. I will remember that your name is holy, and I will honor it with my life.

3. I will remember your day, the Day of the Lord, and how beautiful it is to be with you.

4. I will remember that you gave me my parents; I will respect and love them with gratitude.

5. I will remember that life is your most precious gift, and I will respect every living creature, especially the most weak and vulnerable.

6. I will remember that real love is faithful and pure, and I will keep the promises I make.

7. I will remember to recognize what belongs to others and treat their things with respect.

8. I will remember that words are important and powerful, and I will use them kindly and for good.

9. I will remember to respect other people's relationships, attentions, and affection.

10. I will remember that my value comes from the love I give, and not from what I possess.

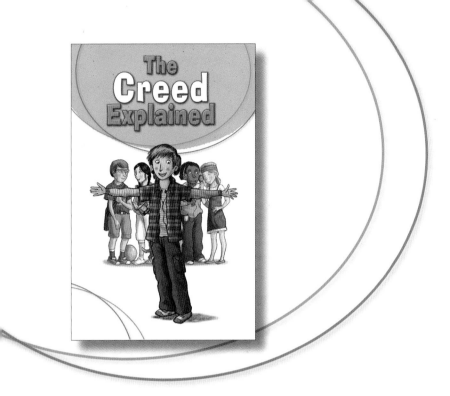

Finally, an explanation of the Apostles' Creed that kids can relate to and adults can rely on!

Explore the meaning of the Creed via Scripture, the *Catechism of the Catholic Church* and the writings of the Fathers of the Church, along with discussion questions that relate to the lives of children. This is a "must have" for parents and teachers who want to share the core essentials of the faith with children ages 8–12.